Kangaroos have Joeys

Barefoot Books

PO Box 95

Kingswood

Bristol

BS15 5BH

This book has been printed on 100% acid-free paper

Graphic design by Design/Section

First published in Great Britain in 1996 by Barefoot Books Ltd

ISBN 1 898000 39 5

British Library Cataloguing-in-Publication Data.

A catalogue record for this book is available from the British Library

KANGAROOS HAVE JOEYS

Philippa-Alys Browne

BAREFOOT BOOKS

BATH

Cod have codlings

Penguins have chicks

Moose have calves

Rabbits have kits

Seals have pups

Pigs have piglets

Deer have fawns

Eagles have eaglets

Dragonflies have nymphs

Ducks have ducklings

Otters have whelps

Geese have goslings

Kangeroos have joeys

Tigers have tiger cubs

Beavers have kittens

Wolves have wolf cubs

Frogs have tadpoles

Swans have cygnets

Pigeons have squabs

Hares have leverets

Trout have fry

Horses have foals

Goats have kids

And moles have – moles!

NOTES

COD

The cod is a fish of which there are 150 species. The Atlantic cod is round-bodied, and can be up to 150 cm (6 ft) long and weigh up to 90 kg (200 lb). There is no marked difference between the sexes. They mature in 4–5 years, at which time they move to spawning grounds for the first 3 months of the year.

The females shed up to 6 million eggs into the sea. These are fertilised by the milt of the males, then they float to the surface of the water where they hatch into larvae in approximately 15 days. The larvae feed off plankton and grow from 0.5 cm (½ inch) to just under 2.5 cm (1 inch). At this stage, the larvae move down to the ocean floor and feed off small crustaceans, crabs and other sea life.

As the larvae grow, they move to deeper water. At 2 years, the young cod will measure about 45 cm (1½ ft) long and will keep together in groups, often to be seen sheltering among the tentacles and under the protective umbrella of a large blue jellyfish. It is at this stage that they are known as 'codlings'.

PENGUINS

Penguins are flightless marine birds, of which the largest species is the emperor penguin. This bird can stand up to 90 cm (3 ft) and weigh 45 kg (100 lb). It is found around the coastal regions of the Antarctic.

In April and May, the penguins congregate in rookeries and begin courting by showing off their bright-orange ear patches. Each female lays one large egg which is carried on the feet and kept warm under a fold of skin. Initially the egg is passed from the male to the female as they take turns to incubate it. After a few days, the female moves away from the rookery to feed at sea, leaving the male to look after the egg for the next 2 months.

By August, when the chicks are hatching, the females start returning. They do not necessarily return to their original mate but search around for a male that will let them nurture his chick. At this stage, the emaciated male, deprived of food for 2 months, will go off to feast at sea while the female feeds the chick with fish from her crop. If a female does not tend to the baby immediately after it hatches, the male is able to provide some nourishment from a fluid secreted from the lining of his stomach.

As the chicks grow older, they come out from under the flap of skin of the adult to congregate in crèches. The parents are then free to go and collect food, so the chicks grow rapidly. By 6 months, they are showing adult plumage and have started to leave the rookery to fend for themselves.

MOOSE

Moose are mammals; they are the largest living deer, standing up to 240 cm (8 ft) at the shoulder and weighing 810 kg (1800 lb). They tend to be solitary and are found in the wooded areas of Alaska, Canada and the Rocky Mountains in western North America.

The breeding season is from September to October, during which time the bulls spar with their antlers. A bull will mate with several cows and then can remain with one cow until the calf is 10 days old. The gestation period of a cow is from 20–22 months. She will generally produce two calves, although a young cow will often have only one.

The young calf will stay close to its mother for the first 3 weeks, becoming more adventurous over time. The calf will remain with its mother for 2 years, by which time it is sexually mature. However, when a new calf is born the following spring, the yearling calf is driven to graze on the edge of the cow's territory.

RABBITS

A rabbit is a mammal. There are about 13 species of cottontail rabbits, varying in length from 25–45 cm (10–18 inches) and weighing between 0.40–2.25 kg (14 oz to 5 lb). Cottontail rabbits in various forms can be found from southern Canada to South America, as far south as Argentina and Paraguay. Most of the species prefer to live in open woodland and bush.

The breeding season is from February to September but can occur all year round in places where conditions are favourable. After mating, the male is driven away, leaving the female to rear the litter alone. The gestation period is one month, after which up to 7 babies (kits) are born, naked and blind. They are placed in a shallow nest scraped out of the ground by the mother and lined with grass and fur plucked from her chest. The mother sits over the nest so that the kits are kept warm and can be suckled with ease.

After 2 weeks, the kits are well grown and able to leave the nest to feed on grass and young leaves. At 3 weeks old, the kits are mature and will set out on their own. The mother will already have mated again within a few hours of their birth, so she may have up to 5 litters a year.

SEALS

Seals are marine mammals. The common seal can measure up to 180 cm (6 ft) long. Its hind flipper being used for swimming, the seal crawls over land assisted only by its fore flippers. The common seal is found mainly in 'colonies' around the shores of the northern oceans, although occasionally it goes up river. It prefers to live in estuaries and inlets.

The common seal spends the winter away from the mainland, returning to established breeding areas in the spring. After 7½ months, in May and June, the pups are born on sandbanks or in tidal pools. The cow nuzzles her pup, breathing in its scent so she may later identify it in the crowd of other youngsters in the colony.

As soon as it is born, the pup can swim. For the first few days it will float with its mother in the water near the shore, and with her help it will swim ashore. Suckling then takes place for 3 weeks, during which time the calf matures and learns to look after itself. The mother then leaves to look for a bull with which to mate.

PIGS

A pig is a mammal. There are 2 main species of pig – the European and Chinese wild pig – and it is from these that the domestic pig is derived. The European wild pig can be as long as 180 cm (6 ft) and stand up to 90 cm (3 ft) at the shoulder, weighing as much as 180 kg (400 lb) in the case of a boar or 135 kg (300 lb) for a sow. It lives in Europe, Asia, Indonesia and North Africa, preferring open woodland with access to mud wallows, and is generally found in family groups.

The sow comes into season every 3 weeks and, when conditions are favourable, she produces a litter of up to 12 piglets after a gestation period of about 4 months. The piglets are delivered one by one into a rough grassy nest prepared by the sow. Using a ring of sensitive whiskers around its snout, each piglet locates a nipple. The piglets gradually start nibbling on roots, grass and insects, becoming fully weaned at around 3 months. The boar takes no part in the care of the young. The piglets are sexually mature at 18 months and reach full size after 5–6 years. One sow may have as many as 3 litters in 2 years.

DEER

Deer are mammals. There are a number of species of deer and one of the most attractive is the fallow deer which is common throughout Europe and has been introduced to North America. These deer are often seen grazing in clearings or on the edge of woodland. The buck stands up to 90 cm (3 ft) at the shoulder, while the doe measures 15 cm (6 inches) or so less. Only the buck has antlers.

Rutting takes place in October, during which time the male marks out a territory. The fawns are born away from the herd in late May or early June. Each doe produces one fawn (or, very rarely, two) which she nurtures away from the herd until the fawn is able to run with her. It stays with her for up to 2 years, by which time it is grazing with the rest of the herd and, if it is male, its antlers will be sprouting.

EAGLES

The African fish eagle is a bird and one of the handsomest, if not one of the biggest, species of eagle, measuring 62–73 cm (25–29 inches) in length and weighing up to 2.5 kg (5.5 lb). It is found near the shore line all over Africa south of the Sahara.

At the start of the breeding season, individuals call to one another and can be seen courting as they soar through the air. Each pair builds a nest of sticks, reeds and matted grass in a tall tree. Usually not more than 2 eggs are laid, sometimes as early as May, but more often in July and August. They are incubated by the female for about 6 weeks.

When the eaglets hatch out, they are covered in white down and fed by their parents on a diet of fish. After 2 weeks, their feathers start to sprout and after 9 weeks they move out of the nest on to nearby branches where they perch and exercise their wings. At 10 weeks old, they are able to fly and start learning to hunt for themselves.

DRAGONFLIES

Dragonflies are insects and many species of dragonfly are found throughout the world. The sky-blue dragonfly is a species common to East Africa, occurring as far north as Ethiopia and as far south as Cape Province in South Africa. It generally lives near streams, rivers or lakes, where it captures and eats other insects.

Both the male and female dragonfly measure about 5 cm (2 inches) long with a wing span of 9 cm (3½ inches). Mating occurs around January or February when the pair can be seen flying in tandem, the male clasping the female behind the head. After a while, they settle on grass or a branch and fertilisation takes place. The female dragonfly then flies off to lay her eggs. With her abdomen touching the surface of a pond or any still water, she releases the eggs which sink until they come to rest in the mud at the bottom of the pond. After about 3 weeks, the eggs hatch into nymphs.

The nymph, which is generally about 4 cm (1½ inches) long with small undeveloped wings, creeps about the floor of the pond feeding off larvae and other tiny creatures. The nymph's main breathing mechanism, situated near the rectum, receives oxygen from small amounts of water that circulate continually through this opening. If in danger, the nymph can suck extra water into its abdomen then quickly release it, producing a jet-propelling effect to help it escape at high speed.

In the course of its development, the nymph can cast its skin up to 15 times, becoming a little larger each time. This process takes about a year, after which the nymph crawls out of the water on to a reed or piece of grass where it undergoes its final moult before becoming an adult dragonfly.

DUCKS

Ducks are birds. There are many species of duck but the mallard is considered to be the ancestor of the modern domesticated bird. The drake is about 60 cm (2 ft) long and weighs 1.13 kg (2½ lb); the female (or 'duck') is usually smaller. The mallard duck lives in Europe, Asia, Central America and the Arctic Circle for the breeding season. In the autumn, it moves south.

After a complex courtship, ducks form pairs. The female builds her nest in a shallow bowl of grass and leaves, lined with feathers. The drake plays no part in the care of the young. Around 10–12 eggs are laid at any time from March to October and are incubated for 3–4 weeks.

When the ducklings are hatched, they are covered in a yellowish down mottled with brown. They grow quickly, feeding off vegetation and insect grubs on land and in the water. After 2 months, the ducklings are fully fledged and ready to leave the vigilant protection of their mother.

OTTERS

Otters are mammals. There are a numbers of species but they are all quite similar. The common European otter can be found across Europe and parts of Asia. Including its tail, this otter can reach 165 cm (5½ ft) in length and weigh up to 12.15 kg (27 lb). The dog otter is bigger than the bitch. This type of otter lives by the river and is an exceptionally good swimmer. It is generally solitary except during mating, and it mates in water at any time of the year, though mainly in spring and summer. After a gestation period of about 2 months, up to 2 whelps are born, blind and toothless.

During the first 8 weeks, the whelps stay in the nest and feed from their mother. She will gradually introduce them to a diet of fish, birds, small mammals and frogs. When the whelps start to leave the nest, the female otter coaxes them into the water for their first swim and teaches them how to hunt for themselves, but they will only leave her when she goes off to mate again – when they are about a year old.

GEESE

Geese are birds. One of the largest species is the Canada goose, which can weigh up to 4.5 kg (10 lb), with a wing span of 195 cm (6½ ft). It is found living near water in Alaska, Canada and other parts of North America. During the winter it migrates south. Outside the breeding season, Canada geese tend to live in groups of up to 200 birds.

These birds mate for life, and early in the spring the goose and gander arrive at the breeding areas in pairs. However, a courtship act still takes place and a clutch of 6–8 eggs are laid in a nest in the ground or away from the flood water in trees and high banks. The female incubates the eggs for about a month while the gander stands guard.

For the first few days the newly hatched goslings are protected by the sheltering wings of their mother. They are then escorted to the water by both parents and taught where to find the most succulent vegetation to feed from. At 6 weeks, the goslings are fully grown and ready to join the flock to find lifetime partners of their own.

KANGAROOS

Kangaroos are mammals. One of the best known of the five species of kangaroo is the great grey. The male, or 'boomer', can reach a height of 180 cm (6 ft) and weigh up to 90 kg (200 lb). This type of kangaroo is mainly found in open bushland in eastern Australia.

Kangaroos breed throughout the year. Just over a month after mating, an embryo, still in its protective sac, is born. The tiny creature crawls through the fur of the female, or 'flyer', to the pouch where it latches on to a teat and feeds. At this stage, the newborn kangaroo weighs no more than 27g (1/35 oz).

After 8 months, a new embryo reaches the pouch, at which point the older joey will weigh nearly 4.5 kg (10 lb) and be evicted by its mother. However, it will still graze near its mother and dip into the pouch to suckle, feeding from a teat that gives creamier milk than that taken by the growing embryo. The joey is fully weaned after a year when it will be ready to leave the protection of its mother and seek its position as a young adult member of the kangaroo herd, which usually consists of about 12 animals.

TIGERS

Tigers are mammals and one of the largest species of cat. There may be variations in size, colouring and markings between tigers living in different geographical regions, but they all belong to the same species. On average, a male tiger can weigh 275 kg (500 lb) and stand 90 cm (3 ft) at the shoulder. These cats are now found only in Asia in habitats varying from rocky mountains to tropical jungle, and they are generally solitary. A female starts to breed when she is about 3 years old, and she meets up with a male only when she is in season. This pairing lasts just for 2 weeks and occurs from November–March. The gestation period is approximately 4 weeks, at the end of which 3–4 cubs are born.

The tiger cubs are born blind and helpless but they grow rapidly. Their eyes open after 2 weeks and they are weaned by 6 weeks. They learn from their mother how to hunt, so that at 7 weeks they can already kill for themselves. The tigers become totally independent from their mothers only when they have reached 2 years, and are fully grown a year later.

BEAVERS

The beaver is a mammal and the second-largest living rodent. It measures up to 105 cm (3½ ft) long, including the tail, and can weigh up to 31.5 kg (70 lb). Beavers are found throughout Europe and North America. They live in colonies of up to 12 individuals in a water 'lodge' built of sticks and mud, or in a burrow on a river bank.

Beavers mate for life and the male participates in the care of the young, or kittens, of which 1–8 are born after a gestation period of 2–4 months. The kittens have soft fur and their eyes are open at birth. They feed from their mother for up to a month, after which they start eating the bark of trees. However, they are not fully weaned until 6 weeks. A new litter is born when the kittens are a year old, but they remain with their parents until they are evicted from the burrow at 2 years of age, when they are ready to go out in search of mates of their own.

WOLVES

The wolf is a mammal and considered to be the possible ancestor of the modern dog. There are 3 species of wolf: the timber (grey), red and the prairie. The timber wolf is the largest and is found in unexploited open country and forests in northern Europe, Asia and North America. It averages 90 cm (3 ft) in height, at the shoulder, and weighs up to 67.5 kg (150 lb).

Wolves usually roam about in family groups or packs of up to 36 individuals. The pack is led by a breeding pair that are thought to mate for life. Breeding normally occurs from January to March, with a gestation period of just over 2 months.

The female prepares a nest in a tree hollow, burrow or abandoned den. She gives birth to 5–14 wolf cubs. Blind at birth, their eyes open after 8 days and by 18 months they are weaned and well grown. Other members of the pack help to raise the young and both parents teach them to hunt. After 2 years, the female is fully grown, the male after 3, at which stage they are ready to take up their adult position in the pack.

FROGS

Frogs are amphibians. As the name suggests, the common frog is widely encountered throughout Europe and non-tropical Asia. This type of frog tends to vary in colour and size but generally does not grow longer than 6 cm (2½ inches).

When not breeding, the common frog lives a solitary life on land in damp places. After the winter, usually from February onwards, it comes out of hibernation and makes its way to water to spawn. The male frog clasps the female around the belly and, as the female releases the eggs, the male fertilises them. Up to 2 thousand eggs can be released at a time.

The jelly-wrapped eggs float on the surface of the water and in about 2 weeks the tadpoles develop and start to feed on small organisms and plants. Gradually their external gills become internal, their hind legs begin to develop, then their forelegs, and finally their tails become absorbed into their bodies. At this stage, the tadpole has become a fully fledged froglet, measuring about 1 cm (½ inch). Feeding on slugs, snails and insects, the froglets will grown and reach sexual maturity after 3 years.

SWANS

Swans are birds. Of the 6 species perhaps the most familiar is the mute swan, which is indigenous to Europe and Asia and has been introduced to North America and Australia. This type of swan measures up to 150 cm (5 ft) long, including its neck, and can weigh as much as 15.75 kg (35 lb). It is quiet compared to other swans as it does not have a distinctive call. However, in many ways 'mute' is a misnomer as the swan can be heard grunting when swimming or hissing when disturbed.

Mute swans live and nest near water, where they feed off plants and small creatures such as fish, tadpoles and insects. Occasionally they live in colonies but usually a breeding pair, which mates for life, will establish a separate territory where it will nest each year.

The nest is a large round mass of twigs and grass hollowed out in the middle. It is usually found among reeds or on a small island in the river. In spring, 5–7 eggs are laid which are incubated mainly by the female, or 'pen', but the male, or 'cob', takes over when she needs to feed. After 5 weeks, the cygnets hatch out.

Swans are often seen swimming as a family unit with the pen leading. They remain together for about 5 months, by which time the cygnets are fully fledged and ready to find their own way.

PIGEONS

Pigeons are birds. There are many species but one of the most common European varieties is the wood pigeon. It can measure up to 40 cm (16 inches) long and weigh about 0.45 kg (1 lb). Wood pigeons live in flocks mainly in wooded areas where they feed off seeds, nuts, berries and leaves.

At any time from April to September, a courting pair of birds will separate from the main flock and begin a complex mating dance. They build their nest, usually a rather frail structure, in any kind of tree. The female normally lays 2 eggs which are incubated by both parents for about 18 days.

The newly hatched squabs are covered in a sparse pale down. For about 5 days they feed exclusively on a substance known as 'pigeon milk' which is produced in the parents' crops. The young are then gradually introduced to solid food such as seeds and vegetation. They are able to look after themselves at about a month.

HARES

Hares are mammals. The scrub hare is a species found largely in central and southern Africa where it inhabits open country and woodland. On average this type of hare will be 52 cm (21 inches) long and weigh up to 1.58 kg (3½ lb).

Hares are mainly solitary creatures and often nocturnal. They breed throughout the year, and the male, or buck, takes no part in the rearing of the young. After a gestation period of about a month, up to 3 leverets are born under the cover of thick vegetation. Their eyes are open at birth and they have good use of their legs. The doe, or female, hare suckles the babies until they are fully weaned on to vegetable matter and able to fend for themselves. This usually takes about a month.

TROUT

A trout is a fish of which there are about 7 species. The European brown trout vary in colour and weight depending on whether they inhabit the sea, rivers or lakes. Despite this, they all belong to one species native to the northern hemisphere , although they have been introduced to other parts of the world.

Trout like to live in cool, fresh water. However, the sea trout, which is the largest in this species, measuring up to 120 cm (4 ft) long and weighing up to 13.5 kg (30 lb), migrates back to sea after spawning up river.

The male trout begins breeding when it reaches maturity at 2 years, the female at 3. This usually takes place in running water from October to February. For spawning, the fish return to the rivers where they were hatched. The female deposits her eggs in a shallow dip in the river bed made by the flicking of her tail. The male then positions himself above the eggs to carry out fertilisation. The female remains slightly in front and to the side of the male while this takes place.

At the end of 6 weeks, the eggs hatch. The fry are 1–2.5 cm (½–1 inch) long. The yolk sac is absorbed by the sixth week, at which stage the little fish live on a diet of aquatic larvae which they continue to eat until they are mature when they feed on insects and small fish.

HORSES

Horses are mammals. They were domesticated up to 4,000 years ago so there are only small pockets of truly wild horses left. However, domesticated horses have returned to the wild in many places: for example, the Mustangs in North America, the Bumbies in Australia, and the New Forest, Exmoor and Dartmoor ponies in Britain.

The New Forest ponies live in herds on grassy plains. On average, they stand 13 hands (130 cm/4 ft 4 inches) at the shoulder and weigh about 270–360 kg (600–800 lb).

Mating generally occurs in spring or when conditions are favourable. The foal is born about 11 months later and is suckled by the mare until it is mature enough to feed totally on grass and to assume a position in the herd's hierarchy, which is dominated by the 'boss' stallion. The foal reaches full maturity after about 4 years.

GOATS

Goats are mammals. There are 5 species of wild goat; the common wild goat, from which the domestic goat is derived, occurs throughout southern Europe, Turkey and Iran to Pakistan. This type of goat stands about 90 cm (3 ft) at the shoulder and weighs up to 117 kg (260 lb). It browses in herds of up to 20 members, led by an old female, or nanny, goat.

Mating usually occurs in the autumn and one or sometimes 2 kids are born about 6 months later. The young are able to run and climb shortly after birth. They reach sexual maturity at 12 months, by which time they are no longer being suckled and are feeding mainly on leaves and twigs. By 2 years, the kids are fully mature, at which point a female becomes known as a nanny goat and the male as a billy goat.

MOLES

Moles are mammals. The best-known species in the northern hemisphere is the European mole. It is found across Europe and Asia and is generally 14 cm (5 ½ inches) long, including its tail. It lives in tunnels underground and feeds mainly on earthworms.

The boar and sow moles remain together only for mating, which takes place in early spring. Approximately 6 weeks later, 2–7 babies are born, blind, pink and naked. After 2 weeks, their fur begins to grow and their eyes open a week later. The baby moles suckle hungrily and by the third week their weight has increased from 2.8g (1/10 oz) at birth to 56.7g (2 oz). At 5 weeks, the young moles leave the nest and they are fully mature by the end of the first year of their lives.